CW00859958

Fragmented Dreams

By Rayaan Ali

Copyright © 2017 Rayaan Ali

All rights reserved.

ISBN: 1974691446
ISBN-13: 978-1974691449

May Allah swt allow you S. to do all the things you couldn't do in this life, in the Gardens of Paradise. Ameen.

CONTENTS

Thank you

I would like to begin by saying thank you for giving birth. Raising me to grow blissfully on this Earth. Blossoming alongside my sisters and brothers. I thank you, my Mother.
I thank you for striving endlessly. Providing with such effort that in my eyes is legendary. These pressures you carry is something I harbour. I thank you, my Father.
I thank you Tezar, for being the best role model that inspired me. It is your character and intelligence that has aspired me.
I thank you Shilpa, for being the older sister that I do not possess. Offering me care and guidance for my success.
I thank you Kamzy, Imran, Umut and Antonio, for existing in my sourest times. Motivating me to thrive; inspiring these rhymes.
I thank you S.B, for being so significant in my development. A precious blessing that elevated me in my element.
And I thank everyone that has ever supported me, family, friends & supporters.
Without any of you, I wouldn't be in the position I am now, therefore, I am forever grateful.

Fragmented Dreams

Fragmented Dreams

A collection of poetry that illustrates life for what it truly is. Portraying imagery in the reader's mind to understand the fragility of living. These poems will take the reader on a journey of pain and suffering, but it will provide the hope that is necessary to prevail over pain. Rebuilding on the tragedies that have overwhelmed hearts and souls. These Fragmented Dreams are fragments of hope and agony. But, to surpass these barriers that are presented before us, you must Find No Enemy.

ME, MYSELF & I

Poetry –

These words are an expression which is my profession. It's an obsession that gives me progression. It bleeds colourlessly because it requires no creed. Yet it breeds at speed but not due to greed. Simply as it breathes the atmosphere on my sleeves. It perceives emotion elegantly and it reassuringly relieves. The feather dipped in ink can scream the weather. Dream of luxurious leather despite being attached to a metallic tether. This speech can provide relief from ghastly grief. Spread a conscious chief's basic belief. If manipulated maliciously it can leave it incorrectly illustrated. Simplistically sophisticated regardless it can be stimulated. A heart is empty until a mother fills it aplenty. Just like how any language doesn't cost a penny. Words brought me a globe of hope to cope. Broadening my scope sincerely so I could reattach the rope. Each word painting a thousand pictures that are raining. Potent scriptures; the blind obtaining eyes that are sustaining. The deaf with ears that last to hear a worded atmosphere. Paragraphs shouldering each tear to embrace any fear. This is a form of intelligent movement that's relevant. Benevolent with development this is an element. Poetic from the start and poetically smart. Poetry is my art and I am a poet at heart.

Me, Myself & I –

Loneliness has been my greatest friend. It's kind of funny, like it'll always be there from the beginning till the end. I'm just talking to myself because that's all I have sometimes. Me, myself and I; as well as these wonderful rhymes. It kept me company when I was stuck in conflict. Reminding me what it feels like to be alone when I lose my instincts. I forget what it feels like to have no one. Because I envision having my own daughters and sons. Despite all of the people in my life, it can still feel like no one is there. Because we tackle our struggles alone and it can be too much to bare. I know what it feels like to be lonely, yet again I don't know. It's difficult to explain and understand but I feel it when I'm low. A companion of the emptiness that has a place inside. When you hear no voices and you just want to hide. Even though these feelings feel repeated. Loneliness can be defeated.

Kareem Inspired a Dream –

Kareem inspired a dream; I now initiate my personal poetic regime. My passion is extreme, just listen to these words scream. Unknown to you; you changed my perspective to become effective. Protective of my poetry but diligently dissecting like a detective. Soundtrack to the Struggle healed my tragic trouble. Popping my bubble so that I can become subtle. Juggling mixed emotions during political commotion. Once frozen like assets; liquidated to continue my motion. Rhythmically hinted humility with intrinsic imagery. I listened instinctively because you spoke vivid validity. I still stumble due to stupidity but 'My Soul' made me humble. Simba's growing up refusing to tumble so he can leave this jungle. There will be a million more just like me joining this war. For every poor civilian, we will no longer ignore. Change starts with the people, not the leader; so, help the feeble. Justice for all; to be equal knock the steeple. Everything I am has still yet to build me into a king. I sling rocks like Palestinians; death is not synonymous with spring. The other side is greener; injustice makes me meaner. I'm listening to the screamers because I too am a dreamer. Wishing for peace and unity to strengthen our community. Musically this message has gained total immunity. Essentially, I continue to attentively study your legacy. Impeccably increasing my integrity; you left me with an identity.

Behind My Painted Smile –

Behind my painted smile, is an obscure vile file. Forbidden deeds, a lack of style with emotions left hostile. Beneath my crooked smile is a maimed lion that needs to be tamed. Ashamed, unclaimed and internally inflamed. Injustice against my name and horror hidden behind the frame. Insane due to years of knowledge with anger that I contain. A broken Britain and lost colonies that are crime ridden. Mindless audacity; written history placed with a ribbon. A mystery to the masses as trickery is used to portray victory. Lashes full of years of iniquity, however that's not misery. False sympathy won't answer the crying symphony. Typically defining my deficiency in another shattered soliloquy. Explicitly engaged but you miss my chipped calligraphy. Initially increasing hostility but pain truly highlights fragility. Resorting to delinquency because I feel I'm correct consistently. Negativity then continues to drain my capability deliberately. The result of innocent anguish and self-imprisonment. An immigrant amongst two cultures has left me vigilant. Ignore pessimism; it's not significant so don't be ambivalent. A bitter sweet predicament can leave you magnificent. Humble yourself, don't crumble when you stumble. Stand defiant in this jungle when obstacles cause you to fumble.

Not Normal –

I'm not normal, I'm far from formal; simply abnormal. Eternally nocturnal and I apologise for when I'm informal. An old soul; yet still a future awaits to unfold. I uphold principle because my soul can't be sold. I'll continue to misbehave as I won't conform to be a corporate slave. Raves don't appeal to me; I waive it because I'm not brave. Neither am I egotistical; humility taught me not to be typical. Instead these clinical words make me feel mystical. Typing my story to myself due to the lack of glory. But that can get gory so quarry my inventory. That is if you need guidance in a moment of silence. Shattering violence can be repelled without science. Escaping the system and constantly seeking wisdom. Building my kingdom before searching for income. I spend time to be socially aware so I know why the world is unfair. I care, I dare you to go against the grain to make this world fair. You can stare and complain while the world causes you pain. Or retain your domain and explain why you won't restrain. It's bizarre; like me, but that's how you shine like a star. Cliché; although without using a car being different can get you far. I know, I'm not the same, not even the average savage. As I'm too busy repairing the ravages of the middle passage. I will surpass my past; forsaking the forecast to pass. I'm not broken glass, but I'm delicate; I'm in a different class.

Isolation –

It's hard to explain, all this pain. It's a continuous chain that slowly drives me insane. I can't express it because I've kept it isolated, as if my confidence has been annihilated. No one understands and no one listens, I feel so ashamed to ask for a hand. Others only see the surface, and think everything is perfect; but it's just a deception so you don't have any negative perceptions. Asking questions to myself for all my selfish projections. Looking for answers to this devilish depression. Lessons are never learned but my bridges are burned. Trapping me on an island of isolation, as if I landed in a hell haven for sedation.

I Am a Mistake –

These earthquakes are so devastating, but I am responsible for my mistakes. Accelerating harshly, I should have hit the brakes. To avoid breaks in the sequence but the damage is done and it aches. All of these choices, yet I let myself become poisoned by all of these voices. They influence these poor actions, opening the cracks. Destroying any potential factions, stabbing my back. I am foolishly repeating the cycle, purposely defeating myself. Naïvely decimating a chance to succeed in completing myself. I need to stop, dropping all of these setbacks. Each time I lose a piece of me that I will never get back. Ruing the mistakes, I am a mistake, mistaken for a masterpiece when I am the master of never finding peace.

Turn Back Time Part 1 –

Living in this nightmare daily with no peace, and it's been so hard lately. No daydream to avoid these acid attacks. Paying for the consequences of the past, there is no opportunity to relax. The scars are permanent; thus, this agony will never leave. Plastered with pain, the wounds will never breathe. Impossible to heal the way I feel, I don't want to be trapped in this ordeal anymore. However, these regrets keep my soul sore. I wish I could turn back the hand of time because every action has felt like a crime.

Turn Back Time Part 2 –

I want to turn back time because I made wrong choices. I got confused amongst all the nasty noises. All I've done is bring myself shame. Painting an ugly picture over my name. I regret every single thing, I doubt my existence. I can never forget anything, I no longer have any resistance. Instead of resisting reality; the truth is what I have come to terms with. Firm in acceptance that anything good about me is a myth. Disappointing every person that I love. I just want to be taken away above. Into the clouds to drift into the distance; a forgotten memory. I want the bottom of the ocean to be my cemetery. I wish I didn't make my own decisions. Because each one has resulted in this position.

Foolish –

I love you and I hate you. I don't want to imitate you. Attracted to your appearance yet in the end I just wanted a humble disappearance. I won't lie it felt like it was easier to die than make you cry. Never did I want to be another part of your past, I really did have hope for us to last. But life comes at you so fast. Maybe it was a long-term infatuation that had mutations of what I thought was love. It was love, but I simply had enough. Enough of what I became, because I was just no longer the same. Broken hopes and dreams, I became a boulder that crushed us. A fatality that was unknowingly unjust.

Complicated –

Loving myself is complicated because the love has been confiscated. Contemplating suicide because not once have I felt content with my being. Seeing flaws upon the floors of myself, failing to appreciate the feelings that resonate. Desolated in despair, the engine has become impossible to repair. Servicing a broken pipe dream that's screaming for some reassurance. However, finding my purpose has only devolved deterrence from the heart to the soul. But there's a lack of matter in the middle so how am I supposed to solve life's riddles?

Cold Blooded –

I've become so cold,
maybe it's age making
me grow colder.
The older I get,
the bolder I become,
because I'm too numb to care.
Is it rare to be so cold blooded?
Maybe it's a good thing,
as I've developed the ability
to block out the pain.
Yet, it comes back like thunder,
a storm of emotions taking me
down under.

Misguided –

I can't guide you when I need guidance.
A misguided soul that's at war with
internal tyrants. Constantly violent, so
the norm is to be numb to the sirens.
Alarmingly quiet but this riot needs
suppression otherwise I will never learn
my lesson.

Misunderstood –

As a male, I can say we're positioned to be carefully conditioned. Imprisoned with misogynistic thoughts that are envisioned. Striving for an agenda so we can appeal to 'Brenda'. Attempting to be the superior gender; how could we possibly surrender? Stuff like weakness is undermined so we're rough. Men want love as much as women do but we're set up to act tough. Ashamed of it but who are we going to admit it to? I have no clue to why we can't commit to you. We're amorous predators and simpler than metaphors. As the temperature rises we become wretched wrestlers. Can we truly progress? Trying our hardest to be a man. It's not easy to understand us; even we have a plan. Why are men so weak with the audacity to turn the other cheek? If you listened to us speak you'll realise we're each unique. I'm sorry that you're just an object because we lack respect. Subjective when we reflect that perfection is what we expect. Admittedly aggressive and objectively obsessive. Apologies for the repressive regime; it's so depressive. Full of lust which leaves you in disgust. But eventually we try to be just because we want your trust. Maturity is medicine, so love us when we become gentlemen. Ladies, love us when we become gentlemen, as we can be genuine.

Second Chance –

I wish I had a second chance and I'm not asking for a second dance. I regret all these glances because it led to a pointless advance. The forecasts predicted storms and I forgot that I'm fragile like glass. My class is worth nothing; I should be trimmed like rest of the grass. So unfaithful; the blood on my soul is so distasteful. Disgustingly disgraceful; now what does it mean to be faithful? Hateful of my appearance as I lack perseverance. Life insurance isn't literal so I should have been grateful of interference. I was never born winning, like so many I was born sinning. Hindsight from the beginning would have stopped my soul spinning. No one should ever follow me, it'll only make you hollow. You'll wallow in pleasure failing to realise what not to swallow. Making dumb decisions; placing myself in an insecure position. A collision course of catastrophe where I've lost my vision. Forgive me Lord for being selfish, I was bored. I ignored your message, I realised selflessness is adored. Young and reckless; I've lost a necklace. I'm like a headless chicken; clearly feebly feckless. A life with regret, how could I forget that I'm a threat? Upset with myself, but to many I'm in debt. I appreciate the helping hand, even if you didn't understand. I wish I never planned ahead, because my plans never land. An idea can sail away so that it's simply a fairy tale. I inhale too much smoke, so I choke when I fail. I've become so vain, again it's difficult to explain. Trapped in a cycle of pain with a generation headed down the drain.

That's Not Me –

I didn't want to be rejected by a culture so I transformed to be accepted. I felt like I was elected into this alien group acting like I was connected. I started off on the small things to thicken the string. Soon to be pulling people with a rope I felt like a ring leader, I was a king. Mesmerised by money that the darkness is where I'd reside. Maliciously misguide my men, they weren't the only ones I supplied. A suspect is what I was, idiotically I began to inject. Subject to turning humans into objects because I had respect. I used to smoke till I choke as I treated everything as a joke. Thus, I'd soak in sins as my body acted before I spoke. I had to express my wealth recklessly to impress. This was what success meant and you can tell that life was a mess. Intoxicating insidiously was the lifestyle with females only in my proximity. But on the other hand, act pugnaciously as blood would rage viciously. However, I would play the game at night and sell stones during the day. I didn't need to pray, I'd just slay and I wouldn't hesitate to spray. Eventually imprisoning myself with a harness because I'm heartless. Regardless, I'm reduced to nothing and I've lost my fortress. The point is you can't duck under the problems; eventually you don't have luck. You can cluck like a chicken and remain stuck. And now I want to be buried in the sea like a villain and repent on my knees. Now I don't know where I should be but for the record that's not me.

Shoes –

Put yourself in my shoes, walk these treacherous miles. Suffer the tragedy with me, maybe you'll understand why the abuse has reduced my smiles. It hurts, burning the soles of my soul. Each step disintegrates the layers to stop me from being whole. These jagged rocks cut through into my skin. Whilst the sun beams heat into the earth so I burn from each sin. I drown in the salty tears because there is no longer an outer layer. Flooded in the littered streets, I've memorised the details; I should be a surveyor. Slain by the dysentery infested slums. Intoxicated on the surface whilst the insides become numb. Because I'm no longer insulated. The blood that's trickling out paints a picture, but the story isn't illustrated. Numb to the cold but the heat is torturous. Wearing the ugliest shoes, but perhaps these are the most virtuous. Teaching lessons of a lifetime. For once, the cuts and blisters are worth it because the results are sublime.

I Understand –

I just want to give back what you gave to me, I want to be able to provide for you. You struggled so I could live. You forgave me when I would misbehave. And it took me so long to understand why you stand. Maybe you were too generous because they became treacherous. Abusing your trust; they acted unjust. But how can I blame you when they gave birth to your name? It was your duty to fund their livelihood that's why you were sent to this country for good. I don't appreciate your struggle enough; how rough it must have been, all the trouble you faced, but the love never left its place.

A Shame –

It's sad that I'll miss your graceful development.
Growing into your element. Being the beautiful child
that you are. And passing you the torch to travel
far. Striving towards the brightness. Thriving in
complete politeness. An attitude that will win over
hearts and minds. A personality that will positively
affect mankind. Sparking empowerment in the
people. Pushing an agenda to everyone to
acknowledge we are all equals. I want to be your
role model and teacher. A guide that listens unlike
a preacher. However, regardless of whatever you
do, I will be proud. You have the ability to lead the
crowd. Shining through the thickest of clouds.
Because even though you're young, I know that the
passion in your heart is loud.

Everything I Am –

Accept me for everything I am,
for my glories and my flaws.
Listen to my stories and allow
me to share what's in store.
Ignore my mistakes and focus
on my present. Everyone breaks,
forgive me, for I try my best to
be pleasant.

Feelings –

Your feelings mean nothing to me so I can be care free. Bare no stress, relaxing with no waves in the sea. No tides to take me away or erode my consciousness. Walking anonymously through the streets so it doesn't ruin my confidence. I abolished your feelings because I am an apologist. Your judicial system is evidently a state of lawlessness. To selflessly throw myself in front of the bus for your feelings would interrupt my flawlessness. An arrogant consequence which I don't shy away from because I despise pompousness. As selfish as it may sound, for once I feel my feelings should mean the most. Because I am not bound to anyone, I am my own host.

Transforming –

I need to run away from everything, for my sanity. To seek significant clarity in my humanity. I need space to realise the flaws under my mask. The face that's covered in imperfections; please don't ask. I struggle to accept myself so how can I expect you to accept me. Ironically, I'd rather you reject me. As I said, I need to change what I have become. Change the fact that from me, there is no good to come. Numb to emotion, yet the pressure makes my blood boil. Ruining any attempts at leisure; it's a curse that repeatedly spoils. Efforts to transform is always met with rejection, like Corbyn for the masses. Addicted to the indifference of life, because this pessimistic outlook is sweeter than molasses. Maybe just one day, I'll be free like untouched civilisations. Living with no shackles; complete untainted liberation. But there's one thing I need to do to reach that stage. I really must transform into a better being to turn to the final page.

Fragmented
Heart

Fell Apart Part 1 –

I thought I knew love, but clearly, I was wrong.
Moving with lust, I was an unjust child all along.
Giving you all my time and affection. It's just a
shame, that heartbreak wasn't within my detection.
Two different cultures, I thought I could make this
work; so incredibly immature. Ignorant to the
differences, allowing myself to become impure.
Too young with narrow vision, I didn't see the
collapse coming. Putting myself in a sinful position,
if only I saw what I was becoming. If only I realised
sooner, your eyes were elsewhere. Once I
witnessed the aftermath I fell into despair. Lost the
will to care, because this pain felt like it was too
much to bare. However, I installed new software
and began to prepare. Regenerating this new me,
becoming a better being. Learning to live with
reality and understand feelings. Growing stronger,
but sadly, strength isn't eternal. Thus, I wasn't
prepared for the next hurdle.

Fell Apart Part 2 -

You took interest in what I considered worthless. I saw your message, I was so nervous. Loneliness consumed me so I pursued you on purpose. Infatuated with your character, I fell for the surface. Building such a beautiful bond - the highest of skyscrapers. Little did I know that it would burn to ashes like paper. Becoming the best of friends, ironically that came to an end. Of course, that was agonising because I didn't expect the love to descend. Families created ties, but I dealt it severance. Pressurised marriage slowly became filled with malevolence. Threatening to leave to the point I no longer wanted to breathe. Smiling on the surface but that would make me misperceive. Scrutinising my every action, I could never relax. Constant critical analysis, not once did you think of the impacts. Conditioning me to be quiet, so with each outburst I'd want to riot. Eventually it got to the point that I had enough and I needed to diet. I lost my mind and myself so I would choke myself to sleep. Popping pills because the wound really did get that deep. I became a stranger to you, myself and everyone else. Bottling up the reality, not realising there is a limit to how much you can suppress. I had to end what we had for my sanity. Because I was in so much agony, it was heavier than gravity. I was becoming a casualty as I was falling into insanity. Living so anxiously, I developed a broken mentality. I regret letting it go too far, but that's what happens when you become isolated. Trapped inside a paradox, my emotions were dominated. I did this for the best of us, because I didn't want to hurt you anymore. I knew you would be happier without me, because I was an ongoing war that was toxic from the core. I was done doing things to my detriment. And here I stand again, trying to go back to my element.

Lose You –

I didn't want to lose you,
but I did the inevitable and lost you.
I apologise if my words
unintentionally abused you,
I didn't realise the pain would exhaust you.
A structural holocaust of emotions;
with each motion having a detrimental cost.
Did I lose you?
Of course, I did, as each pause
was another bullet to coat the sugar with blood.
And I'm wearing it, as I drown in this flood.

Forgive Me –

Forgive me, I regret breaking you apart. I get that I played your soul and burnt your heart. Having fun with the fire, I guess my false promises made me a liar. I let the situation become dire, wearing you out like a tire. Not once did I bring us in for a pit stop. Supplying broken ladders; I failed to anticipate the split drop. The multiple falls, I was deaf to your calls for help. Every time we would restart, I'd stall myself. I'll admit, I was too troubled to hurt you. Too in love with you to even alert you. Thus, I am to blame for letting you die. Losing this game, I am the reason you cry. It's a shame you couldn't trust me, but that's my fault. Unable to be just to you, serving you assault. Deep further into the sealed wounds. Destroying the petals before they bloomed. I initiated the seduction of your sanity by placing an injunction. I am the destruction; the cause of your malicious malfunction.

Falling –

Falling,
again and again,
never will I learn.
Falling for you just
so I can internally burn.
Capturing the wrong feelings
in the wrong season.
Intoxicated in self-pity despite
the self-induced treason.
I said I wouldn't do it again,
but I guess I'm a sucker for pain.
I want the sun yet I hate it like the rain.

I Think About You Sometimes –

I think about you sometimes, wondering if I did the right thing. Pondering over what it means to make my heart sing. I question whether it was just an illusion. I ask if what I thought was love was a delusion. I think about you sometimes, I feel like I did what was best. Letting go of everything I contained in my chest. Without me, your life is actually blessed. Whilst we were with each other we were constantly stressed. Perhaps our future was just a false dream. I guess we were in the wrong team. There was a lack of communication. Consistently complicated because we lacked cooperation. But would things have been different? If only we didn't act so belligerent. Was our future really in our hands or did it just slip? Because we didn't understand so we were bound to trip.

Bury You –

I had to bury you in my mental cemetery. Burning your library because I'm sick of your memories. It was all an illusion which had me living in a dreamland. A delusion before my very eyes and my mind would scream for me to understand. My heart was too naïve as it yearned for affection. A part of it knew that this wasn't perfection. This was a totalitarian nuclear napalm gun. Commanding my every action in a torturous manner like a slave in the sun. Bellowing peace to my heart whilst injecting fear into my mind. These types of crossbows were ready to fire; they were not one of a kind. Existing to rule over gentle personalities. Ignoring any immoralities as they repeat casualties. Breaking me until I broke free. Dissolving the shackles after giving up with my pleas. It was a corruption of the conscience; tainted like an election. It felt like a disease to have such a crumbled connection. Faultier than the wiring inside. Which sadly could no longer connect, but at least we tried. We live on and keep these events in our chamber of secrets. It's a weakness but that's just a part of the sequence.

Change –

People do change like the seasons without reason. In complete secretion and it feels like it's an act of treason. Stunning and cunning leaving you in a state of continuous dreaming. Streaming with emotions, fuming but you try cleaning. Cleansing the mental state which sadly generates hate. The mind debates how to dictate your utopian state. Wishing for psychological security because you lack maturity. The impurity within you demands prosperity. However, without clarity you're caged in this emotive austerity. Leading to increasing insecurity you feel inferiority. A part of you wants to be heartless but you're born with a heart. If only you could start over, although you forget that you're smart. Feeling insufficient; illogically inefficient. Happiness deficient and you struggle to remain beneficent. Calmly collect and reassess yourself so you can reconnect. Resurrect your entity; don't neglect your soul, reflect. Reality may disturb your mentality because it feels like insanity. Don't think of it irrationally; expand on your personality. An intricate incident which has left you indigent. You're innocent to this system so forget that you're impotent. It's temporary like this world, just be yourself. Your health is everything; don't fall into the trap of materialistic wealth. Hold the applause because my entity withdraws. I'll admit, I myself am entirely made of flaws. Stitched together with good intentions. Imperfect; cut the tension so you can reach ascension. Liberated happily so express yourself as this is reiterated. Throughout life, simply let it go and you'll feel exhilarated.

Heavy Heart –

Breathing with this heavy heart; it's so dark. Full of contempt and anguish in parts with no place to park. Following a road so narrow with demons following. Tailing any happiness to do some horrifying hollowing. This heavy heart wants to withdraw from the system. Because it's tired of the brain failing to listen to any wisdom. This heavy heart is filled with heartbreak and pain. Memories that make the heart ache and the mind go insane. This heavy heart is overweight but it's plagued by hunger. Dying for relief from this furious thunder. The heavy heart cares too much making it, its own heartbreaker. It is the brain's worst neighbour. A nightmare that is dying to be alone. A heart that is dying to become unknown.

Issues –

I am human, I have issues. Proven to never end; it can't be wiped away with tissues. I make mistakes and I never learn. Trembling from these earthquakes and this wound burns. These tremors make me stumble along this broken bridge. Terrifying trolls with my temper, but I assure you that's a glitch. Like the Wall Street Crash; some things are bound to be disastrous. Like my mind state, wanting to clear it of any sadness. Emptying out any malice and ridding myself of these dry tears. Attempting to build a palace for my loved ones whilst living with my fears. Despite all the agony and anger, I truly just want to cry. Falling into another fallacy because I miss my family; thus, I lose the will to try.

Unfathomable love –

I need love. I crave it, it is never enough. Because without it, I feel so rough. I am human, just like you, I can be the manliest of men, but I can't deny reality. We can be of the loneliest, that could end up as a casualty. We want to be loved, because affection is beautiful. I feel so enraged at this deep dejection, as I always end up delusional. I want this love, but I hate it like my worst enemy. It feels so damn necessary, but I want to bury you in a cemetery. You're within my grasp like the golden snitch, but you elude me. Stolen away and abused by another Grinch, so it's only right to exclude me.

Trust Me –

Place your trust in me, I'll treat you justly.
Justifying your presence to be necessary
as a must. Never will I judge, I'll only ever
elevate you. Supporting and strengthening
the structure as my faith resonates with you.
But of course, trust must work both ways;
a mutual contract. It can't be viewed
abstractly otherwise the bond won't stay
intact. It needs a solid foundation like a
building, otherwise the top will collapse.
A firm dedication is crucial to fill any gaps.
Actions speak louder than words, thus you
must act on what you say. Only that way,
will the trust stay.

Emancipation –

She came and emancipated me;
two souls now amalgamated.
Eradicating insecurities and
activating areas in the brain for
memories. Connected with our
telepathy we sail in serenity.
Protecting me preciously; she
deals with me delicately.
Becoming a necessity that loves
me indefinitely.

Her –

Her intelligence emphasises her elegance,
Endless in her eloquence, that it doesn't need
evidence.
Her magnificence is unquestionable as she's a
specialist in her elements,
And her preciousness is priceless so you can't be
sceptical of her specialness.
Her affection is majestic; it's a permanent patented
protection,
And the connection we have is rejuvenated all the
time with her passionate protection.
Her essence isn't a treat, but a gift that's not
discrete,
Oh, how she completes me, I'm so thankful that we
could meet.
Her piousness is so admirable, it makes her so
desirable,
She's compatible with my character, now do you
know why she's so valuable?
Her shoulder holds me afloat through the journey
we travel on this boat,
This boat called life; covering her with my coat from
the cold, cliché but take note.
Her soul, her soul, it's so impeccable like her love,
it's a chemical,
Not biology; the chemistry is incredible, but she is
more than respectable.
Her, just her, that's whom I plead for, as I need her,
I just want her to succeed and with her I wish to
share my deeds.

You're More Than Enough –

And you're more than enough in this rough world.
Alleviating the strain on my soul; elevating me
above the pain threshold to keep me whole.
Embellishing my heart with grace and cleansing
any ounce of disturbance from my face.
Nourishing my entity so heavily; you initiated a
flourishing nature like your name within my identity.
Evidently, you're more than enough and I'll forever
reply to that with my love.

My Canvas –

Upon this blank canvas lays a secluded broken
bank,
Filled with shortened planks to cross the atlas with
an empty tank.
Tumbling into a shaking fissure because the belly's
beast is rumbling,
Crumbling my entity as it's difficult to withstand
continuous stumbling.
Distributing emotions so freely like this canvas is an
ocean,
Where I can express explosions within this colossal
commotion.
In a split second, you became a saviour; saving me
from armageddon,
You beckoned to me, then you stared at me and
my cheeks reddened.
My canvas is yours, I share it with you because you
care,
I declare my life to you because my feelings are
only for you to bare.
I've chosen you, my bride to be; my wife, it's within
you that I confide,
You don't misguide me nor do you try to divide.
Now soliloquies don't exist because my heart
dances with you in symmetry,
To a blissful symphony which we write together in
concealed calligraphy.

A Beautiful Discovery –

A beautiful being, beneath and above the surface.
Kind hearted and soulfully living with a purpose.
Adorable in her art, but that's just a start. A
formidable heart that'll never break apart.
Admirably ambitious with a passion that's vicious.
Rising without fail like the sun, she is persistently
auspicious. With a smile that glows brighter than
stars. Displaying an elegant style whilst maintaining
royalty higher than the Tsars. Her laughter became
his greatest discovery. Providing selfless
assistance in his recovery. It's so infectious; a
healthy addiction unlike her love for shoes. But she
cares for him, for he stays within her jurisdiction,
erasing every bruise. It's like human therapy,
inserting purity. Purifying the darkness in
magnificent sincerity. She shoots him down to keep
him humble. Whilst he accompanies her in the
jungle to prevent any stumbles. They saved each
other in a mutual manner. Building a uniquely
unusual bond which could only be planned by The
Best of Planners.

-    S.B x

Joy –

I just want to bring you joy, so you can simply enjoy. Pulling you away for at least a day from all the catastrophes, casualties and tragedies. Casually lighten your dark days, discarding fallacies and bringing to life your fantasies. Because I always cause you so much pain, troubling you like a travesty. But honestly, I'm just trying to please you, your majesty. Forgive me, forgive me, for I just want to live you, obsessively you are my life source as you forever guide me upon the right course. Agonisingly I anger you, not for banter, but out of my own idiocy, hideously harming you but I mean no harm. I'm just trying to charm you to hold my arm as your existence is eternally calming. I always say you're the best blessing I could ever have, but that's difficult addressing how because it's unexplainable. However, possessing the most perfect qualities that are sustainable, so perhaps I can explain it bit by bit on how you fit. Being so virtuous and voluptuous; with a beautiful virtue of patience to deal with me and my impatience. May Allah reward you for your patience, especially in dealing with me, Ameen.

Beautiful Marriage –

Together we tie the knot; not to walk alone anymore, but to be unified into one entity creating a new identity. Baring trials and tribulations; sharing smiles and adulations. Raising the next generation with heavy anticipation breaking limitations. Strengthening each other in all aspects as we empower how we connect. And as one we walk through the passage of life within our beautiful marriage as Husband and Wife to reach the afterlife.

Someone Like You –

Someone like you, you're so heavenly with such incredible chemistry. Endlessly emitting emphatic ecstasy essentially. A necessity to those around you because of your integrity. I wish your entity was everlasting as you have an impeccable identity. Intensively studious and you act angelically. Aesthetically pleasing; teasing me, as you have me gazing attentively. With a magical aura that could care less about capital. Classical in your words which is clearly admirable. Your principles are pivotal putting you at the pinnacle. A formidable companion making you unanimously invincible. You are perfection as you unconditionally shower your affection. Leading me in the right direction so you have my protection. After all the tears, you'll fall into a state of loving laughter. You'd rather be modest as purity is what you harbour. Prosperous in your endeavours despite the pressures. Never severing your smile as it makes the weather. Infused with passion; no one can compete with your fashion. A beautiful attraction that makes you the best distraction. Righteously pious stopping me from acting violently. Silently soulful and we progress privately. Regardless of everything; what we do is timeless. Someone like you to exist is what I wish.

Subsistence –

I think of you during thunder, because you pick me up through each blunder. Under the weather you're forever making me wonder. It's not an illusion that you're the perfect solution. Thus, I've reached the conclusion that only you can make me feel such emotion. Giving me full adoration as I commit complete admiration. You're my stunning salvation and with you I feel liberation. Jointly suffering each struggle, we halt treacherous trouble. Protecting our bubble so it isn't popped by any rubble. You're so pure that you're a blessing I'm so sure. Enlightening my life as my light, a permanent cure that makes me secure. You take away any stain upon me; abolishing pain. You contain only good intentions as you're forever listening to me complain. We strive together, so let's continue to thrive. Making me drive forward, I've never been so alive. Distance doesn't stop anything, what's important is your existence. Perpetual persistence pays off as you are my means of subsistence. Breathing is harder when we're apart, it feels like I'm wheezing. Believing in you is all I can do because you are so relieving. I cling onto you out of love; I wish to be your King. And I'd die to hear you sing, so upon your finger let me place a ring.

Therapy –

I need your love, not these pills.
But this fluoxetine keeps me still.
However, I crave your affection,
a body to keep my reflection.
An abolishment of failures and rejections.
Assuring me of a strong tethered connection.
You have become my therapy,
keeping me calm
by transferring energy to my palm.

New Page –

I don't want to grow up mummy because I'm a dumb dummy. The capricious context of life isn't guaranteed to be auspicious. Rather it's a vicious cycle that will sedate any sense of ambitiousness; I can taste the malicious behaviour in the air. That nature alone I struggle to bare. I'd rather take a detour back to my infancy because I'm not ready to mature into the infantry. I am not a secure soldier. I am too insecure but that's not shown on the surface. But I'm perfect to you and her. In your eyes, I will always be your son regardless so I understand why you say "No" and that's not because you're heartless. And that's why it's now her duty to make me into a man; to breathe beauty into my being. Bringing the next stage into fruition; you can happily watch as with your permission she'll help me turn to the next page.

Thank You –

I am so grateful, for keeping me alive. Blessed by my best teacher for being taught how to survive. Especially in this world where we constantly suffer. You've always been in my heart to help me recover. Despite my naivety and foolishness, you support me. Tackling and battling the demons, through this battlefield you escort me. Giving me the power to lift you higher. The most beautiful being, without you, this art isn't something I would be able to acquire. You have faith in me, especially when I have none left. Keeping my soul safe, you deserve rest. I could never repay you, but it's my turn to try. I had to learn the hard way, and I never want to see you cry. Because you've been through so much pain. Just take it easy please, you don't need to strain. Don't worry for me, just elevate the others, the way you raised me. Speak of them just as you praised me. Loving them the way you love me, my sisters and brothers. I am forever grateful, that you are, my mother.

Open Letter –

Mother I love you, and I know I'll never understand your pain. I need you, I don't think you're insane. I'm sorry for the drama that I've caused. I'm grateful, for your love, I hope it's never paused. You taught me well, never did you put me through hell. Yes, I did rebel but you only wish for me to excel. Criticising me constructively, making me punctually productive. Initially instructive till now and I try not to be disruptive. You faced so much mental and physical affliction which is hidden in the past. It isn't fiction because I've heard the scars in your voice, but I never asked. I wish you had a better life, I wish I had the courage to say this. But here it is in an open letter, I should encourage myself to say this. I know you believe in me that's why each time I come back it gets harder to leave. Tears fall as I'm grieving, but I receive your love and for you I'll achieve. I appreciate your existence, I swear your beauty will never depreciate. If only I could alleviate your suffering, but I promise I'll never deviate. I always had the nerve to disturb you but now I envision giving you what you deserve. You always observe my sadness and a place in my heart for you is what I reserve. It hurts to see you in agony but I know it'll be taken away by Allah. So, my Duas are for you, because the least I can do is get you to Jannah.

My Best Friend –

My beautiful sister, you're my best friend. You're too young to understand but that bond will never end. The best blessing that God ever blessed me with. For her, I have everything to give. You're so cheeky and devious. Making fun from a situation that is tedious. Your beautiful savage behaviour is applauded. Everyone adores it as if you should be awarded. Providing everyone with genuine laughter. A comedic prankster creating her own disasters. She's always grinning bringing everyone happiness that's so genuine. Bringing love to the heart as blissful medicine.

Secret Trusts –

I have your secrets hidden within my chest with an unsolvable algorithm. I've held it on trust permanently, isolating it like my mannerisms. It was a gift to me based on your will, but still I kept it a secret as there are no beneficiaries. I guess this level of loyalty is compulsory from fiduciaries. Your pain is still mine, I kept it to remind me that below the surface things are not fine. The misery and happiness, your sins and your deeds, it is a chapter that only I'll ever read. No one else can see those pages, no matter what age I reach. I won't seek any gain as these principles are strict like Boardman. I just wish you'll be able to forgive me for slaughtering you like a swordsman.

Hopeful Heart –

I said I wouldn't search, but I'm chasing you. Envisioning a future with you; embracing you. Never did I think I could find a being like you. No one else could invoke these feelings like you. All my energies are reserved for you. I want all of these memories to be preserved by you. Sitting in silence staring at the sun setting. A private getaway from the struggle that we are never forgetting. You are my peace amongst the violence. A beautiful guideline granting me guidance. Because of you, I wish to better myself. Increasing the longevity by taking care of our health. Feeding it the fruits of trust and truth. Planting the seeds carefully to create our own youth. I love you for your flaws and perfections. Because every part of you is precious, from your purpose to your imperfections.

Broken Heart –

This heart is aching from all this guilt. It's covered in cracks, it doesn't want to be rebuilt. It doesn't want to open up to trust anymore. Because evil is everywhere, nothing is just anymore. A negative perspective of a broken heart. You could call it trust issues, but the issues are rooted from the start. Deep within the core that pumps the blood. I'll repeat this again, that it is stuck in a flood. Struggling to comprehend people. Lost like a plane in an ocean because engagement is lethal. Maybe the cure doesn't exist for this boy. Perhaps he's just an IMF scheme portraying hope that deceitfully destroys.

Used & Abused –

Sacrificial, for you because I'm so selfless.
Beneficial to you because I don't know how to be
selfish. Responding to your every text in seconds.
As if it's a test to avoid you getting hurt by my own
weapons. Allowing my life to revolve around yours.
Just so you can evolve; so, light can surround you.
Helping you fight your own demons. Doing this
without any good reason. Working for you until I
could no longer walk. Letting you walk all over me
so I could no longer talk. Exploiting me like natural
resources in the Congo. Beating me senseless until
the skin bursts on this bongo. Used until I've
become worthless. Abused for your own gains on
purpose. Draining me without giving anything back.
Raining curses upon me when you can't
understand why I attack. Slashing at your fake
affection. Done with your deception, thus I'll serve
you a dish of rejection. Not once did you
appreciate, leaving me confused. Used and abused
till I became internally bruised.

Demonic
Dreams

The Darkest of Hearts –

A heart lies within this chest, falsely treasured when it's darker than the darkest days. Darker than an unlit closed cave. Collapsed in, crushing one side until it's become numb like Obito. But even the darkest of hearts have a part untouched from the darkness. Because light never vanishes, it only ever grows, even if it becomes smaller than a pin drop. The dark heart just needs a little love to make the dark arts stop.

Sinful Addiction –

Accustomed to sinful sensations. Falling tragically for these treacherous temptations. It follows me, as well as leading me to the demons. Different tricks, but they feed me the same seasons. They know that these games will leave me inflicted. Infected with a disease, evidently, I am addicted. Sweeter than the aspartame in my soft drinks. Exterminating my brain cells carefully so I fail to think. Sinking into a pit of evil so I can drown. Because to sin has become as normal as a frown. Slipping into the snake's mouth as I fall further down. My conscience becomes heavier than poverty tax. Crying whilst I smile to conceal the impacts. I face withdrawal symptoms as I avoid the enticement. But my environment is a permanent advertisement. Telling myself, just this last time, it's fine. Repeating the cycle, the next day and feeling like I should resign.

The Devil –

You drive me crazy with temptations yet seduce me to be lazy. Ross's prima facie duties are so hazy whilst the future is intoxicatingly wavy. You embrace me with aspartame, just so you can disgrace me. I wish I could eternally erase and displace you, but you misplace me. Jailed selectively for a month with some tape, but the whispers still escape. He instigates rape whilst eradicating little red riding hoods and her capes. Stimulated destruction through commercialised corruption. Illustrating ill instructions innocently with reckless methods of reproduction. Spreading sinister sterilisation and extinguishing civilisations. Initiating British South African concentration camps and Dominicans deporting Haitians. To some he is the professor but, he is the oppressor. The suppressor of good and every war's aggressor. Burning the trees to take further pleasure in killing the bees. Hindering humanity with disease and creating amputees. Leopold saw mutilating the Congolese as one of his duties overseas. Like General Gordon teaching the Sudanese a lesson as there was land to seize. The evil this entity emits is forever implemented through another identity. From greedy coke chemistry to pointless jealousy. Obvious yet you're oblivious to the backbite you do each night. The white man's stereotypes continue to the enemy's delight. So many choose to dance with the devil and some try to jump off from his level. Enticing you to wrestle a losing battle so that you become a vessel. Maybe the world would be a better place without the devil's demons in this space. If we embrace love surely, we can win this race.

Bad influences –

Surrounding me to make sure the eye contact
never ends. Distorting the path ahead, making my
journey bend. These bad influences try to hold onto
my conscience. Reiterating that every bad thing is
simply nonsense. Obnoxious to the light so the
darkness is my companion. Infiltrating the good in
me and making an expansion. I try to run away
from the bad but it drags me back. Tags in another
demon to pursue the next attack. All of these drugs
wish to elevate me. Sedating my health; the only
thing it'll do is negate me. All this negativity tries to
throw me into the abyss. I resist as much as I can,
even when these sins ask for a kiss. Yet I let the
verbal pollution pollute me. Constructing a false me
as others refute me. I could have followed the
wrong crowd. Sheepishly slaughter myself and be
proud. Live in a bubble that I'll never withdraw from.
But I hold moral law close; principles that aren't
numb. Now, it's a must to keep the good in my
vicinity. Because the light has always been a
special affinity.

Voiceless Part 1 –

Am I voiceless? Do I have no voice due to the lack of choice? Am I supposed to rejoice when I see a Rolls Royce? Being commercial isn't intrinsic; I was born controversial. There's no reversal because it's an instinct not a rehearsal. With time, the Earth's showers are turning sour as we cower. Would you bring flowers if I jumped off a tower in my final hour? You don't believe me because my words empower those who grieve. They deceive you to achieve an agenda that makes you misperceive. So, I leave repeatedly as they cheat me and beat me. But I'm not alone, so they can't delete me or defeat me. Treat me as an equal as I deserve to be heard, even if it's absurd. Your vision may be blurred but your ears can't be deferred. Sometimes I break down because it's hard to remain awake. I do this for your sake, yet I find myself questioning if I'm fake? Am I just too serious? Why is everything so mysterious? Are my demands imperious? Maybe I'm just delirious? Maybe I should suppress my views because they're not true. These dreams I pursue need to come under review. I should just remain plain as being different is hard to maintain. I abstain from this campaign because it's dying in vein.

Voiceless Part 2 –

Do I have an objective? Is life really so subjective?
I'm not a detective but this system is infective. My
reflection is yourself; do you see the connection? A
natural selection; a beautifully misguided collection.
Chasing material desires until eventually our input
retires. Eroding like tires, no one cares when
someone's soul expires. Shackles tame us; trapped
in an eternal game. Can I claim that only shame is
placed upon my name? Will you speak for me when
I become too weak? In these bleak times, please
don't turn the other cheek. Because I Can't
Breathe; I clench my fist whilst I grit my teeth. Look
beneath the story or there will never be any relief.
Don't choke me, I bring peace despite being broke.
I spoke too soon, justice is nothing but a joke.
Hands Up, Don't Shoot; I'm far from a brute. I can't
salute a tainted flag and a thief in a suit. Don't just
stand there, doing nothing is unjust. I don't trust the
people in power because they'll let me rust. Scared
of what you think of me so I'm bound to not make a
sound. I found my thoughts to be stuck
underground. Silence is golden but it's worse than
the violence. It's the worst form of defence;
evidently an offence. This fussing is pointless;
ignore what I'm discussing. It's something
meaningless because I'm nothing.

Voiceless Part 3 –

If these walls could talk which way would you choose to walk? Would you draw on the board with chalk? Look for prey like a hawk? What would you think? Would you let yourself sink? Would you smoke and drink till you hit the brink? Would you have sought after the divine thought? Or will you be professionally taught not to get caught? From the beginning, you can't hide the fact that you've been sinning. Indefinitely swimming in fire, so ask yourself then if you're really winning? Don't be a Naughty Boy for the cake, no one likes a snake. Unless you're a serpent, being fake will be rewarded with a stake. Unconditional allegiance isn't worth losing for a couple of pence. You might gain another sense so don't jump the fence. So, do you really want to see my vision? You can't comprehend what I envision. You'd fall into a prison if you were in my position. You'd beg for an escape after witnessing systematic rape. Your nails would scrape the chambers that are covered in blood tape. Forgotten like the sterilisation of the black civilisation. Ongoing in the Indian population via cancerous radiation. But I can ensure that your voice will be drowned out by the noise. Don't throw your toys out of the pram because the drones search and destroys. This is modern warfare; don't relax, you best prepare. Beware of the elitist's enforcers as the result is despair.

Out of Touch –

I'm out of touch, because my goals are not within reach. Unable to change gears with this broken clutch because I overreach. It's worn out like my soul. The fuel is running out like coal. It's unknown whether this position is sustainable. Because the toxins are not containable. Understanding is now unattainable. Lost in the mist and that isn't explainable. Feelings don't make sense when you can't comprehend your own senses. Thus, the result is to build feeble fences. Isolating each incident intentionally. Concealing it like an immigrant to remain indefinitely. I'm out of touch with people like severed ties. Because the knot won't stay intact when the bond dies. Whilst I worry about this futile fact. I forget I'm out of touch with myself as I've lost all contact.

Hate Myself –

Apparently, I'm always negative, maybe it's because I'm sensitive. In an immoral insensitive world, you can't expect someone to be positive. Feeling like a caged convict in constant conflict. Evict these emotions because I'm an anxious addict. My mind state is unpredictable and no it isn't pitiful. The restlessness is visible and no this isn't fictional. Hatred towards myself because I'm a criminal that's unforgivable. Disgustingly despicable, I pointlessly forget my principles. Sinisterly subjected unnecessarily, so I feel disconnected. So much is expected of me that I constantly feel rejected. It's difficult to please people so my entity is never at ease. Is this a disease inflicted upon me so that my existence will cease? I guess I have some violent issues, maybe I just need some tissues. Battling eternally like Mogadishu; I should learn jujitsu. Because I'm being attacked literally by demons for no reason. Abusing the lack of cohesion, to the point my account is close to deletion. Horrendous homicidal thoughts have disturbed me so I feel sporadically suicidal. If only a tidal wave could take me away because my life's not vital. Drowning like Bangladesh, I'm perishing like Gilgamesh. I need to refresh myself to remember I'm still alive in the flesh. I really have come to hate myself but this is a test of faith. I guess it doesn't hurt to love yourself, regardless I ask the Lord to keep me safe.

Selfish Complaining –

I have the audacity to complain when I don't recognise your pain. Unnecessarily I feel like I'm wrapped in trouble but then yet again you're trapped in struggle. Struggling to survive but you aren't even alive. Yearning for my bed, however you're wishing you weren't dead. You warn me not to be like you because it'll come back to haunt me when people taunt me.

Problem –

I have a problem, I never knew it was that until it created other issues. I condemn it because it leads to sadness and tissues. Selfishness is the root of it or maybe it's restlessness. It's effectiveness on my wellbeing deteriorated my attentiveness. In the past, it was minimal just like at the start. But as I drowned it would last and sometimes cause a surging blast. I became a disastrous danger, far from a life changer. I'd endanger those in my proximity regardless of whether you were a stranger. Is it genetic or conditioned? Because sometimes I feel imprisoned. Like the sanity within was partitioned and detrimentally decommissioned. But I hurt the one I love the most with this curse; a type of pain I can't reverse. Permanently pessimistic that I'll do worse so it's best I lay my head in a hearse. I apologise; but I beat myself to the core and cover with a disguise. And the anguish lies in my blood, so I just hope it dies. Never learning my lesson, thus I try to live with discretion. And that fails too; orchestrating self-imposed oppression; so, I ask questions. Like will I ever reach ascension with this antagonistic aggression? And why does that lead to regression of my being and capricious depression? Don't sympathise, I just want to rid myself of this disease. It took far too long to recognise, sadly struggling to remain at ease. This all retreats radically with no hope for its defeat. So, as it depletes, the trigger becomes engaged and the cycle repeats.

Bleeding –

Why can't I stop bleeding?
These demons just keep breeding.
I'm shrieking in agony,
because my power is depleting.
Repeating the routine,
my soul is the only thing I'm conceding.
Because I've already lost it all,
I've already taken the fall.
Called upon to take charge,
but I can't march when I'm heartless.
The enemy is at large;
however, the blood is hard to harness.
So, I remain alone, as the ties are cut
so there is no binding bond.
A phone is no longer of any use,
when no one responds once you've been conned.

Immortal –

I am mortal, I will die,
I can't escape this world
through a portal like Quan Chi.
But my spirit survives,
it always will - attacking any oppressor
with the intent to kill.
Being treacherous is reckless,
thus, never will my soul form
a deadly alliance.
Forever following the defiance
of the elite, whilst staying in
complete compliance with the truth.
Despite being bruised,
the message will never be abused
because it is immortal.

Burning Out –

Working these late nights but what's the point when I'm losing sight of my own vision. Losing control of my own position. Filling my pockets resulting in burning a hole in my heart as the sleepless nights tear me apart. Living a nightmare so I can only daydream in the dark; maybe then I might feel like I'm actually making a mark, but I've already lost that creative spark.

Release Me –

Release me from this disease of greed at speed. Please I beg you to spare my creed and honour my deeds. Mislead us; destroying any chance to succeed. I misread each signal; failing to realise what I truly need. Release me of these allegations and twisted temptations. Senseless sensations surround me with negative connotations. Lacking direction; concentration and a set destination. Miseducation of illustrations with illicit implications. Release me from this eternal spell of hell. Why is it hard to tell you that so many people are stuck in a shell? The imprisonment of those born impotent. The militant attitude shown towards the innocent. Pillaged villages are not just a bunch of images. We take our privileges for granted whilst the decimation finishes. Release me from this illusion of confusion. Dreaming of revolution which has led to my exclusion. Chasing temporary materialism; I'm gazing. Embracing reality is difficult with what I'm facing. I won't reach ascension as my heart is racing with ill intentions. My brain is begging for attention but I left it in another dimension. Release me from everything; leave me with a pair of wings. I'm not a king but a product of this system, so what do I have to bring?

Dark
Reality

Dark Reality Part 1 –

I am obscure, concealed in darkness. A premature adult, living multiple personalities so the real me is difficult to harness. The real me is heartless, frighteningly full of iniquity. Imagining sickening imagery, it's with no ambiguity that I lack humility. Let me give you an insight into my wicked thoughts. Internally lacking no remorse because I don't care if I get caught. Starving myself like a Palestinian just to make a statement. My body is bruised and battered, oozing blood from my pores at the bottom of a basement. Gassing myself with cyanide for the hopes of escapement. Mortified by my own urge to kill, I don't want human engagement because I'm tired of emotional enslavement. Using a steel bat to whack myself to sleep. Hoping to knock the sense out of me so I don't weep. No longer wishing to feel or see, I want to be senseless. Defenceless to my own demons, the desire for death is endless. Strangling myself with barbed wire because it's a start to being barbaric. Dangling pure acid drops above my eyes because the smell of burning is aromatic. Blinding my being to the atrocities, I beg for my struggle to go unheard of like a Yemeni child. Trapped in a bubble of lava, adjusting myself for hell because my sinful soul is so wild. This is mild like half of the false flag shootings in France. Whereas the extremes involve losing my legs in Syria due to US drones so I am no longer able to dance. Waterboarded until my blood is replaced with water, just for information that I don't possess. Deafened with screeching till my eardrums explodes and bleed, because that is enjoyable distress. Hopelessly licking the bottom of bins because I'm too busy indulged in sin. Faultlessly a victim to the pharmaceutical industry as I've become corrupted by violins. It's not dark enough, I can still see light, but when this continues, it'll permanently be goodnight.

Dark Reality Part 2 –

And the night only just started, like a crack fiend scavenging for loose change. Just a few pennies for the next crack rock to hit a higher range. Selling kidneys in cholera infested slums of India, because at least I'm not selling bodies. Intoxicating myself by injecting unknown diseases to defeat my own antibodies. Dismantling my muscles to remove the strength like colonising African Kingdoms. Suctioning the structure with structural adjustment programs to create more victims. Economic modern-day warfare - that's IMF induced famines like Somalia. Gruesome self-inflicted conflict like the mutilation of female genitalia. Inserting blue crystals in my intestines to traffic these drugs. Or maybe it'd be more twisted if I used HIV infested plugs. But I've been a child slave for over 19 years. It's just a shame I'm drowning like Ahmed in these tears. Because I'm the type of cockroach that isn't worth saving. Rather, stamp on me with napalm for not behaving. Giving birth to enraged deformities, a colossal calamity. Rolling thunder into my blood stream, screaming at this insanity. Running naked as the napalm burns through to my bones. Like white phosphorus erasing my eyes so I'm blind when I retaliate with stones. Smoked and burned in a giant cladded coffin. Removed from the rich man's sight so often. Because I'm poor, but not as poor as the National Health Service. There's money for war, but none to feed fuel into the furnace. Just sacrifice me in pure ethanol flames at Bohemian Grove. Cooking my rotten carcass over their satanic stove. Before that, infiltrate my system and compromise my organs like the Ottoman Empire. Make sure to electrocute each organ with the highest of volts by attaching copper wire. Or maliciously massacre me a million times like the Mongols. Shaving me with a sword, castrating me and harvesting my body bit by bit into worthless fossils. Lastly, lock me to the floorboards so I can bathe in a mixture of vomit and excrement. If I survive, throw me into the Middle Passage to drown; that would be benevolent. Batter me publicly for speaking out. Hammer my head so my brains are leaking out. Especially when I've called for emergency assistance. Brutality at its finest when there is minimal resistance. Justice is hypocrisy when it's on heroin. Addicted to the dark side so there will never be a heroine. Initiated into the children's militia, gunning down my own mother and father. A ghastly beginning of the dark side that I must permanently harbour. I can firmly admit that I no longer possess any sight. Because my heart has been sealed off from the light.

Murdering Myself –

It's been lingering on my conscience for what seems like eternity. Sickened by my being so I want to cleanse this world of my identity. Feed me until I starve from a famine in Ireland. If only I could deport myself to an island. But a lifelong trip to Madagascar isn't viable. Or you could just shoot me like Trayvon Martin without holding the police liable. Burn my body like the community of Rohingya that has been long forgotten. Whip me until my blood is soaked up by the cotton. Perhaps it would be easier to exterminate me through henchmen. Or just clarify my ethnic cleansing through an international convention. Admit to showering me in white phosphorus. Grab a samurai sword and slice at my oesophagus. Because I don't want to breathe. I want to be the cause of why I will leave. Barricade me behind walls with no access to necessities. Demolish me like a false flag attack to reach new intensities. I'll state it bluntly like the rusty pole pierced into my heart. All these attempts and acts of murder is based on the past. The historical reminiscing of evil that has torn humanity apart. I feel that it is important to remember these injustices because we move on fast. Repeating the same atrocities with no qualms. If we don't learn, then surely the blood remains on our palms. I am the future; however, I am also the past and present. I am losing this test; likely to come last if I don't repent. I killed myself yesterday; I am killing myself today and I will kill myself tomorrow. A lack of change will mean that reality will remain hollow.

Morals are Simply Words –

All this morality.
But it's wasted without clarity.
Weightless principles; lacking gravity.
Humanity is in disguised insanity.
Rules and regulations keep us in control.
Keeping an eye on us with permanent patrol.
But many are above the law.
Prioritising the rich; ignoring the poor.
Becoming corporate cattle is a success.
Articles express that the western blood is what they obsess.
Killing is bad only if it's your kind.
Millennium underdevelopment goals for mankind.
Charitable causes that pay from donations.
Justifiable silenced African amputations.
Vilifying a peaceful ideology.
Because the threat is posed from a foreign economy.
Pets are overfed whilst children starve.
Throwing the people, a bone to carve.
Reducing benefits whilst rising rent prices.
As well as misinterpreting like Isis.
Education is so important but it is for the wealthy.
To live is to be rich but it has become expensive to be healthy.
And to be free is to own the judiciary.
Completing injustices with a malicious mercenary.
Sweatshop slavery makes the world rotate.
And love means nothing in this world of hate.
Emotion has become emotionless due to materialism.
Disrespect is acceptable under the guise of chauvinism.
Nothing matters if it doesn't affect you.

But when you're in trouble you expect everyone to respect you.
Yet again, blood on your hands is the norm.
Desensitised to distress as you've been taught to conform.
The pharmaceutical industry enjoys supplying drugs after drugs.
But the only guilty citizens are so called 'thugs'.

Darkness –

I see nothing but gore and tears on the anonymous floor. Dripping blood stains on the doors of a just war. Lewd lies listed on the wings of a flattened fly. Supply a wicked zion and softly scream my battle cry. Humanity's capacious coffin in a historic oasis. Flirtatious western waste dropped on a regular basis. Orchestrated beheading; burned babies that's upsetting. Silent begging; the futuristic fallacies are what I'm dreading. Peace and violence are synonymous but, yet so autonomous. Victimised to monotonous mornings and we're all homogenous. Zyklon B merged into the atmosphere till you're submerged. Halos practically purged and lucifer has emerged. Cowardly campaigns to contain everyone's remains. Surrounded by flames; mystically a masked magician with games. Dark thoughts, my mind should be sentenced in court. Caught by hatred; I hate myself for what I have been taught. Lacking sharpness, maybe I'm agonisingly artless. Heartless with twisted fantasies a result of my distant darkness.

The Mystery of Iniquity –

The mystery of iniquity is distinctively presented in history. Judiciously aware today unfortunately artistically. Duplicity is politically willingly decreasing fertility. Creating a critically assessing society physically and pitifully. Systematic degradation wickedly ruining one's ethnicity. Sensitivity increases incivility; initiating instability. Immobility becomes intrinsic specifically staged euphemistically. Maliciously mongrels use validity to create their own vicinity. Fittingly this isn't imagery; it is the reality of the ministry. The elite use their authenticity; analytically to abuse our inability. Brilliantly they have us blissfully living in bigotry. Instantly from infancy the industry has us trapped in their infantry. The trinity doesn't have sympathy for victims of this symphony. It was created artificially deliberately, to feed you conditionally. Viciously stripped of virginity; we misinterpret paradise visually. Miserably placed in hell; wittingly we bite the apple deliciously. Humility is a lost cause; cynically we encourage publicity. Additionally, striving for applause and religiously worshipped for stupidity. Clinically cleaning malleability will gain peace plausibility. Realistically we must claim our own responsibility for survivability.

1984 –

Yesterday, the display may suggest this game is for
you to play. Another temporary crazy day that'll
simply fade away. Doublethink is law; blink the
wrong way and you'll be left on the brink. Victory
gin and cabbages; the national drink and stink. The
abolished weak Oldspeak is just an old leak.
Newspeak is the new speech; updated every week.
Tiresome Telescreens trap thoughts to keep you
glum. Numb from the calling for 2 minutes of hate;
you succumb. Mini microphones monitor movement
in bushes like an officer. Goldstein the unpopular
illusion; however, his voice is jocular.
Subconsciously submitting; seductively splitting.
Not quitting resistance is cunning, it's rather
unwitting. Cleverly you disperse your energy to put
yourself in jeopardy. Expertly the Thought Police
contain you tenderly. With distress so you can
confess a false mess. You can't express yourself
as they suppress your sense to dress. Vaporise
your entity; completely erase your identity. As an
enemy, especially because thought is a felony. Life
becomes a mystery through fabricated history.
Iniquity inflicts injury which hinders the chance for
eternal victory. Instructive insanity is injected
because it's destructive. So, you become
constructive to Big Brother; sadly, forever
productive. This is no fantasy, this is falling upon us
rapidly. The reality is that this is relative to modern
day humanity.

Freedom of Speech –

Immune to the toxic they feed you with a spoon.
Sensitive cartoons illustrated by goons. Inciting
hatred by abusing something so sacred. It's no
surprise Paris saw red when they came for their
head. Malleable minds have made the whole world
blind. The consequences are far from kind; that's
how the system was designed. Fear continues to
invade the soul throughout the decades. House
raids are in place and a backlash of grenades.
Kicking an innocent lady who consequentially lost
her baby. Maybe this was to distract you and leave
you shaky. But every action will always cause a
reaction. The media will caption the headlines with
a distraction. Right-wing dehumanisation and
demonisation. The decriminalisation of hatred for
reunification. When you dehumanise a person you
can justify your crime. Because you nullify their
existence as a human with time. Violence is wrong
but so is saying a group of people don't belong.
Staying strong is difficult when you've been
mistreated for so long. There's freedom of speech
and rules that you can breach. Religions teach
peace but they're being assaulted with bleach.
Contradiction lies within the futile system's
affliction. There's no restriction but an agenda that
if it's wrong you'll face crucifixion. Don't oppress my
people please, they shouldn't be expressing
distress. Let my people dress freely because it isn't
to impress. If I'm free to speak then what about
WikiLeaks? Unlike Julian Assange, am I free to
critique the power-hungry freaks? Obama is the
devil and Netanyahu is on another level. That
statement was special; that definitely hit a blood
vessel.

Suffocated –

Alienated animosity amongst us; living in viscosity.
Failing to comprehend the ferocity of this western
monstrosity.
Unspoken atrocities are the common foreign policy.
Monopolised dishonesty bringing generous
democracy.
There's so much hypocrisy within a certain modern
ideology.
Consciously brewing faceless hatred for a lack of
apology.
People suffer so much for the crimes of others.
All due to another malicious magazine cover.
Demonic depictions to coincide with factual fiction.
Evident contradiction but this thirst for bloodshed is
an addiction.
These poor decisions are leading to these vilified
divisions.
An incision on the surface is like a circumcision.
Uncovering the dirt which continues to oppress the
hurt.
Not the first curse; first stain upon this white shirt.
Infrastructure destruction as a result of an eruption.
Televised seduction advising imbecilic instructions.
Bottom of the ladder but Black Lives Matter.
Disillusioned rappers while the brains go splatter.
Black Panther Party protection, Ku Klux Klan
selection.
Pointless elections and countless reflections.
Poison within the core with dark knights in Darfur.
Blood along the door and severed heads upon the
floor.
There's nothing wrong with being a fighter against
vipers.

But why are American Snipers permitted to go
hyper?
Heroes don't kill people, they don't abuse the
feeble.
They destroy needles rather than justify what's
illegal.

Consequential Colonialism –

Colonised and contained, I'm enraged at history.
Imperialised inflicted injections, I'm infuriated at this
iniquity. Taking such beautiful and bountiful land,
only to transform it into barren earth. Giving birth to
hatred and racism, ruining its worth. Dividing
people, the consequences have been so lethal.
Years and years of war, I don't blame them
because you're evil. This western world that I'm in
conflict with. Even now they have the audacity to
restrict freedom; thus, it has become a myth.

Inequality –

My rights have gone missing. And now it feels like it is beyond existing. Lawfully given but unlawfully followed. And any justice is temporarily borrowed. Martin Luther King was extinguished by the state. But that is kept hidden as it would change history's fate. Any threat to the elite white supremacy is decimated instantly. Like Malcolm X, eliminated by the white man's infantry. Every Rosa Parks must sit on the other side. Because they're in fear but the racism isn't something they hide. Mike isn't allowed to run because he'll be gunned down. Whilst the media teach lighter is nicer but that melanin in your skin is your crown. And it isn't simple knife crime if you are Kelso Cochrane. Evident brutal racial hatred that isn't linked to being insane. And I apologise to you Emmet Till. Because lynching still takes places today, thus your blood continues to spill. Lucrative jobs are mainly available to my white colleagues. A white office painted in institutional injustice; it never fails to intrigue. And I will always be the first to be stopped and searched. You will never understand as it is impossible for the roles to be reversed. Maybe you'd understand if an officer bashed you with a stick. Pretending that the system is equal; what a cruel trick. Strangled until you can no longer breathe. Discriminated as drug dealers that function as thieves. Our lives simply don't matter; that is the truth. Shooting us and disarming our youth. Purposely showering us in ignorance so we can't speak. But never will we refuse to be weak. United we stand because they can never take us down like Eric Garner. We won't crumble away as this strength is something we will permanently harbour.

Maybe –

Constant construction, this place is turning into a
jungle that can't function,
Destruction of tranquility due to commercial
corruption.
A result of greed that impedes on humanity's
creeds,
Thus, the future's seeds can't become legacies as
they bleed.
You could say that lucifer has gotten into the
bloodstream or we've just become rotten,
Slowly suffocating in the malleable cotton's coffin.
Maybe a conduction of terror is an orchestrated
eruption?
Simply an introduction of a false flag to cause
further disruption.
Enacting Draconian laws in the name of national
security to start wars,
And make the poor poorer as you rob their nature
stores.
It's insane that they've done it before and they'll do
it again,
Regardless what happened was inhumane, and the
peace will continue not to remain.

Empathy –

The effects of empathising is so powerful, maybe we need to do that more. Because only then to an extent can we understand what people are fighting for. Or conclude why people are a lost cause or feel the pain of an unjust war. There are so many paths to take; six of them like pain, maybe that's the result of war like Nagato. But the difference in your being doesn't stop you from giving up like Naruto. Money is an evil but so is jealousy, just look at Danzo. It's venomous but we can't all wear masks to block it out like Hanzo. I don't care how intelligent you are; in fact, the knowledge is useless if it can't compliment your character. It's like being an unconscious barrister. It's only when we learn to empathise will we truly become one in our humanity.

Rayaan Ali

LSD / Long Shore Drift –

Obliterating tides.
Incinerating insides.
We try to change the Earth but that power isn't
within our range.
Why do you think LSD is so detrimental?
Because we don't understand the experimental
impacts that occur on this sentimental sanctuary.
Destroying habitats and reconstructing landscapes.
Captivating chemicals in the consciousness so the
soul is out of shape.
Whether you conduct it on land or through your
hands, the consequence it looms amongst us with
impending doom.

Trapped but United –

Trapped in technology.
Intoxicated in a venomous ideology.
A poisonous trait.
Deciding our feeble fate.
Lost in fabricated fantasies.
Living to fulfil fallacies.
Giving our energy the wrong way.
Glorifying immorality; we need to pray.
To focus on serenity.
Building a beautiful legacy.
It is our duty to protect.
But we have lost respect.
Destroying our own homes.
Victims of this system; we are clones.
Drones that do not question.
Following blindly without discretion.
Failing to see the catastrophe.
That inhumanity has become normality.
Burning innocent flowers down.
Through the authority of a crown.
Cruelly decimating the soil.
All in the name of sweet blood oil.
Colonial supremacy is a tragedy.
Sheepishly accepting this masked misery.
Lives mean nothing to royalty.
And the people's silence is loyalty.
Supporting the mutation of seeds.
Speaking out when the skin bleeds.
It is too late, it is not enough.
The oppressor has been too rough.
The past is now finished.
But the future has not diminished.
We can change what is tomorrow.
Strength doesn't stop at a plateau.

We do not have to be victims of deceit.
The power is ours, not the elite.
United we must stand.
And together we must hold up high, our hands.

Unique –

Politics or 'Poli-tricks'? Politicians put us in our position. This system decreases our wisdom to listen. Imminent institutional warfare is inimical. To the innocent but the agony is biblical. Our decisions should be our own so don't blame religion. The media is not your vision so let's abolish division. Education will increment the ambition. But question everything about the placed dictations. Society is a demon which sucks out your piety. Staying in a state of sobriety shouldn't give you anxiety. Focus on the reduction of media and government corruption. Materialistic seduction shan't stop this million-man march destruction. There is no pro-white or pro-black, there is only pro-people. Physically we differ but our souls are equal. Each gender should not conform to the media's agenda. Raise your fist as a defender and repeat after me, we shan't surrender. Empower the people because those in control are lethal. Revolutionise the mind, so we can rid this utopia from evil. Speak up against injustice and watch what we accomplish. We can't regress because we'll be wasting a wish. Unify as one because unity will strengthen the community. Beautifully increasing the Earth's futurity suitably. Sustain your smile; I can assure you it's worthwhile. Spreading hope for those that need an extra mile. Hatred will subside to nothing and love will rise. Revise the advice given from the wise. Because human borders are artificial, we are one nation. This union is the idealistic blissful civilisation. Abstain from the lies and break away from the chains. Maintain your freedom; use your brain. Don't turn the other cheek and help the weak. Seek happiness and don't forget to be unique.

Stay Woke –

Wake up, I beg you to stay awake.
Because this system is trying to
snake you, poisoning you to break
you down internally. Whilst they
paint pretty pictures for you
externally. Intoxicating you with
their fiction, they've got the majority
hooked like a television addiction.
Too blind to differentiate between
what is right and wrong so they
continue to play you like an
instrument all along.

Unity –

We need unity but we can't stop the fighting. We
are so uncivilised as we act like it is inviting. Rioting
amongst ourselves, we are injuring each other. This
is not the right way to act tougher. We are hurting
ourselves when we inflict socio-economic violence.
And the real oppressor watches us in silence. A
modern-day tragedy where we are unable to
cooperate. All this knowledge and resources but we
don't know how to operate. Fuelling our egos
through greed and reputation. We are a different
breed; beasts of no nation. We belong to the elite
as their pawns. Falling into their traps and being
crushed in their palms. Genetically modified with
their versions of corn. Becoming unnatural and
inhumane as they cut off our arms. Honestly, we
are the victims of our own chaos. We don't want to
build, we just want to run away to Barbados. When
they come for us all. We will regret, as we will stand
alone as they stand tall.

For the People –

I don't want to be a dictator upon people. I don't want to be a ruler that's lethal. I can be a leader, but I don't want to lead people astray. I don't want to continue the mistakes that has taken our humanity away. I want to help you with love and hope. I want to take away any barrier that prevents us to cope. A better world where hatred is abolished. A place where affection leaves you astonished. Caring for one another; prospering together. Sharing out of love; protecting our seeds from wretched weather. I want to empower each and every one of you because you deserve it. You are anything but worthless; created for a beautiful purpose.

Hopeful Humanity –

We have lost our humanity. After countless years of brutality. It is evident, we don't know what it means to be human anymore. For far too long we have been rotten within the core. We need to love and be generous. We do not need rage in our veins that make us act venomous. My fellow humans, we need unity. The spirit to create a welcoming community. Demolishing borders; truly liberating our movement. Defying dictators' orders; the beginning of improvement. Working for each other, not ourselves. Disregarding wealth and fighting for our health. Together, we can destroy the misery. Demonstrate to the demons that our happiness is not a mystery. It is innate within us; developing as one. Perhaps, we can write a better world for our daughters and sons. If only, we can end this bitter cycle of hatred. Focusing on the stunning things that are sacred. Taking the power away from the greedy. Distributing equality and justice to the needy. Only then, the trees will stop crying. Because they will witness that we are trying.

Fragility

Severance –

It's easier said than done, to be ruthless. After being accustomed to fruitless antics. No longer wanting to be dramatic. It takes time but the approach you take must be pragmatic. Sometimes severing ties is for the best because otherwise you'll be stuck in a knot. Decomposing in a dead end, like a dead tree in an empty forest left to rot. Unnecessary delay will make you lose the plot. Owned by a new host, lost in treacherous land so you're bound to get shot. Implement German efficiency, ruthlessly slaughtering the Brazilians. Because this cup is yours to take in this world of King Williams. Maybe it will hurt at first but the longer you wait, the more of a curse it becomes. But when you realise the pain the person causes you isn't worth it, you'll be numb. Numb to severance, you can give notices or mutually agree. However, just swiftly cut the shackles and you will be free.

Selflessness abused –

Stop being so selfish, to abuse my selflessness. It's a wicked trait of selfishness. Taking advantage of a person's kind nature is absolutely vile behaviour. A person who mistreats generosity deserves no saviours. Not even a single petty favour. Take the first exit on the roundabout and close the door. You don't have to live with the fire inside, some people just need to understand they need to be their own guide. They say life isn't a free ride and there is no magic money tree. The same people will expect your help once you've died, giving your billions to strangers without setting you free.

Lessons –

The reality is, not everyone is supposed to be in your life forever. Every single person in your life will leave you, even your father and your mother. Because every soul shall taste death, and that's never kept away from us. Therefore, expect to lose everyone, because that's the reality. Some people that may seem to be there for the long term, may just be a lesson in this test. Teaching you what needs to be taught before being taken away. Today you confide but tomorrow they may no longer be by your side. Some people are lessons, some are memories and some are a part of you for eternity.

Bridges –

Bridges have burnt, perhaps that is the only reason I have learnt. Learning that people are seasonal, feeling like an atrocity that's unspeakable. Change can seem so shocking but it must be believable. I guess that is normality, yet the range in difference hits hard like insanity.

Growing Up –

It isn't easy to grow up. The thought of all of it
makes you throw up. The trials pile up and
overwhelms. Trembling at the helm but you must
react to this realm. Circumstances destroy you but
you don't have a choice. You mustn't lose your
voice. Each event erodes your existence.
Repeatedly at a rapid rate but you must show
resistance. We all have our own struggles. And it
can feel like there are so many layered bubbles.
Enveloping you so that you can't escape. Covering
your lips with red tape. That isn't an option, you
must persevere. Take control and become the
engineer. Ageing before you have to age. Turning
faster than you can read the page. It can only make
you stronger. Allowing you to thrive for longer.
Unnecessarily tough, but you will feel the rewards.
You must keep slaughtering the situations with your
swords. The chords are yours to play. But it will
always be your decision to stay. To continue
competing with the fiends. Washing away the
harshness until the slate is cleaned. It is cruel,
growing up before you can even grow. But it is a
blessing in disguise that you will never know.

Reality Check –

A painful reality check dished out by my cousin. Hurt and dejected, it felt like a concussion. The repercussions meant that I became confused. As if I was betrayed as a victim of the system; I felt abused. I learnt the hard way, even if it felt harsh. It was necessary so the land didn't become patches of marsh. Drowning before I could even lift off the surface. Clarifying the difficulties of a future without a purpose. Realising things aren't as simple as it seems. Realistically concluding that you can't just follow your dreams. It became a must to keep my options open. And I thank my cousin for the words that were spoken. Preventing a dire ending in a closed off tunnel. Now, I can fight off the system with little to no trouble.

The Strength of the Devil –

The devil is too strong in the way he captivates.
Selling you the sweetest solutions that he always
fabricates. Pushing you closer to the end until there
is no return. Laughing and smiling with you whilst
you burn. Internally hiding the destruction.
Magically making it a mystery when he causes an
eruption. You throw the stones violently to erode
him. Digging deeper till you think you have
burrowed him. But he escapes to bring you back
into his reach. Invalidating your existence even if
you try to impeach. Overthrowing the temptation,
he traumatises you with. Damaging your
conscience till it ostracises you to live. He has you
thinking you can't get any worse. He has taken
control of you like a curse. Yet again, when you're
so far into the light; he exists. And you still fall
because it's difficult to resist.

False Reality –

We could call each other a teacher but we're all just a feature. Surviving spontaneous procedures; surrounded by callous creatures. Oppressed by conditioned natures; contested with failure. Nothing feels major as we live a life full of paper. Antagonistically proceeded; amorous advances impeded. Exceeded expectations but don't think you've surely succeeded. Blind to 'the eye' waiting for the saviour; so, we constrict behaviour. Procrastinating prayer because there's always later. Made from the maker; wishing to see the creator. Asking for favours; lacking unique flavour. Insidiously objective but still strongly subjective. Stupidly selective as the mind is increasingly defective. Reflective of reality; contrasted due to the lack of clarity. Modelling morality to rapidly reduce any incapacity. Practically persistent in a false palace like Alice. Occupied with malice, so drop the chalice. The concern to sustain humanity is a lesson that we must learn. Before the world burns, wisely we must choose our turn.

Emptiness & Failure –

Feeling nothing because there is nothing there. Every emotion evaporated due to despair. Eliminating envisioning a future because it seems futile. Feeble in ambition as disappointment is so brutal. Accustomed to this lack of feeling; it's no longer unusual. Thus, the lack of expression is so suitable. Nothing can rid this corpse of the emptiness. As all of this false filling is laced in deadliness. Accepting it for what it is, because I never behaved. Constructed like the concrete so how can I ever be saved? Used to losing like the person I am; a failure. However, only I can beat the blues and be my own saviour. Never have I met expectations. Exceeding effort endlessly, thus death stays in constant contemplation. It's a shame that this no longer phases me. Because failure has become a curse that faces me. Befriending and elevating my empty soul. Digging deeper until I can no longer fill the hole.

A Generation That Can't Cook –

We live in a generation that can't cook. A generation that would rather watch television than read books. A generation with miseducation that only cares about looks. A generation which won't inspire a nation. A generation that will remain victims in this system. A generation that will forget wisdom. Because no one cares, they'll stop and stare but they don't care. So, it's rare to find a kind soul. A soul that won't break bonds but ignite unity to keep us whole. Am I overthinking? But can you blame me when the land we live on is sinking? Can you blame me when a teenager's culture revolves around drinking? Our generation needs a reality check. Turned back on-course before becoming a wreck. We need a revolution in our generation or it will be a shame. Because if the next generation goes wrong, we have ourselves to blame. We are the examples. Or perhaps we are the shattered samples. We cannot shy away from the problem at hand. This is an issue we need to understand. Feeling the problem hit our hearts before they become numb. It's time to take responsibility for what we have become.

Untold Responsibilities –

Sometimes untold responsibilities fall into our place. Forcing us to mature and embrace. Facing reality early because life handed us the baton first. Feeling like a curse; expecting the worst. Only through the struggle can we excel. Using hidden intel to propel. I know that these responsibilities feel like a burden. Overwhelming you to close the curtain. But God gave you this test because He knows your might. Envisioning that you'll see it as a blessing in your sight. Even if it is strenuous to the point it causes fatigue. Remember it is only ever elevating you into another league.

Like a Star –

You shine so brightly in this crimson red filled night.
In a time of hostility, you haven't lost sight.
Fighting to energise positivity in the sky.
A hope of prosperity for every soul that continues to cry.
Burning so bright, like a star.
Shooting wishes far.
Hearing the souls that wish for relief.
Saving minds from grievous grief.
Expressing as much love as you could possibly shout out.
But like every star, eventually you burn out.

Fake Friends –

Users, that have two faces; the abusers of people, that won't think twice about switching spaces. Ingratiating behaviour to condition you with false affection which isn't portrayed in their reflection. Kisses upon your face whilst ripping up your back to pieces before they replace you. It's a shame that the serpent doesn't reach the surface until you witness how they abuse your trust, disgrace your name yet tell you you're perfect. Fake friends are the snakes that deceive you to try and cause your end.

A New Beginning –

It wasn't easy but I left the only place that was truly home. A sanctuary like the Eden Project; my own protective dome. Leaving behind my Queen and first love. Living without the blood in my system became tough. Weakening every bond in that beloved building. Demolished slowly; a slow death like flowers wilting. Flushing away the foundations to my peace. Separating my soul between multiple places; no wonder I lost a piece. Isolated away from my loveable siblings. It feels like an ending despite this new beginning. It deteriorated my state of mind. And every positive part of me fell behind. Unable to think straight as I became uncomfortable. Misunderstood by myself as my mind became ungovernable. Missing everything that kept me driven. I was slowing down like this broken Britain. An eclipse took over my eyes and I lost my vision. I lost myself as my purpose became hidden.

Fragmented
Dysfunction

Mentally Reckless –

Mentally reckless,
my soul has become
woefully restless.
Battling temptation,
telling myself I can't give
into this selfish sensation.
Because I have responsibilities,
so I have no right
to take my life regardless
of the strife.
But I'm so weak,
I struggle to speak to myself;
crumbling like a tower,
that is the state of my health.
Shoot me,
refute my existence
because this is a pitiful resistance.

Forget You –

How could I forget you? Because I'm perpetually in debt to you. Undoubtedly, I regret, as you changed me, you rearranged my emotions to cause mental commotion. A detrimental chemical reaction that ignited a short-lived flame, but it was fundamental in telling me that nothing was the same. All these objects are you, because I was subject to your abuse; I object to this, I won't reflect on the pain anymore. Egotistical as it may seem, however right now I need to focus on myself, because being selfless to you hurt; like an everlasting curse that's agitating, and now I'm exterminating you at the end of this verse.

Angry –

I'm so angry,
I wish someone
would hang me,
out to dry because
I'm soaked in gasoline.
A machine
that's susceptible
to vindictive viruses.
A highly flammable
obscene vaccine waiting
to infiltrate the cracks like roots.
Destruction from the foundations
like when a war minister executes attacks.
Burnt out dead wood that's prepared
to simultaneously combust oneself,
because why live when the world
is unjust and unwilling to help.

Weighted –

I want to be alone, trapped in my own thoughts. Knots tied in my throat and veins so that the blood clots. I've come to hate company because it boils my anxiety. I know I'm not fit for society, especially when I lack piety. I don't want nervousness to poison my mind anymore. I want to find a purpose for my malnourished core. Besides worshipping God, I don't know which path to take. Because not much remains real to the eye so I try to stay awake. But I just want to weep myself to sleep. Our lives have become so cheap; thus, we're thrown down deep. Mentally I can no longer handle the tragedies. Constant casualties and disregarded formalities. I want to turn off and turn away from the light. Running away into the darkness because I've lost the will to fight.

Seasonal Cycle –

The winter waves sorrows into my hollow corpse. Reminding me of the empty void that no one will fill. The long sinister nights excite the demons, encouraging them to kill. Demonstrating the delusion, we're fixated upon, attacking the blind spot we've created. Once the last line of defence falls in November, the bare skin is exposed. And the deep infiltration is instigated in another attempt to decapitate the body before the armour is refortified. And we March again until the following Winter, repeating the cycle until we meet death.

Nothing to Give –

Eyes closed and hands
in my pocket because
I have nothing to give.
A noose and a tie
because it's easier
not to live. Fill the room
with cyanide smoke so
it's easier to choke.
I have everything to lose
but I'm already broke.
And I'm on my last legs
as the top is due to
collapse. Running in the
same circuit resulting in
a relapse.

Guilty –

I can't stop the guilt, because life can't be rebuilt. I said I'd visit, but I left it too late, the cruel reality of fate. I wish I saw you at peace but instead you were inflicted with a disease. My patience was anything but a virtue but obviously you were too young for it to hurt you. Instead, I watched you leave, dealing with the whole process I don't think I had the chance to grieve. Standing by your father in his time of need because your passing made him perpetually bleed. But I thank God, for once your expression wasn't one of agony despite the lack of vitality. Even now, I tell myself I'll visit but I delay it as I replay the situation. Forever left in a state of constant contemplation.

Regretful Tragedy –

Your pain was my pain, a pain that was never slain. Hurting harder than a whack from a cane. Your beautiful tears that would fall would affect my conscience so gravely. I just wish you left this world more safely. It's pitiful, I am only full of wishes and regret. I didn't give you time, I didn't pick you up and I didn't see you enough; I will never forget. I watched your final moments that broke me. You were in excruciating suffering, each time I witnessed it, it would choke me. Struggling to breathe in absolute agony. Never will I witness a more heartbreaking tragedy. Slowly you lost your movements and then your sight. But the will to live was a constant fight. Staring into your eyes, I could never lose your soul. But closure will never bring composure, this is just something that you cannot console. The machines just kept breaking and I couldn't look. Because I saw the end coming like a book. You were leaving us, and I couldn't comprehend that with your lack of breathing. Your soul left too quickly before I could even utter your name. And to this day, and forever on, will I hold myself to blame. Resting in the Garden of Peace, the only time you've finally been at ease. Even though you've departed, the love will never cease. And I hope you're doing all the things you couldn't do in this life. Walking, talking and playing with no strife. It was inevitable that your death would create a void. One that can never be filled because death is something we cannot avoid. I am grateful that your suffering has ended and that your soul has gracefully ascended, but May Allah swt grant your parents peace. Ameen.

22/02/17 –

I got too brave, thinking I could save you. But I was too late and that just happens to be fate. I blinked and instantly my heart sinked. And I feel like I should quit because I delayed every visit. It will be the only regret that I can never accept. Because you can't rewind time to ease the horrors in the mind. And never will I find tranquility over this issue despite all the tear stained tissues. But it will always hurt to say your name because living will never be the same.

Imran's Friend –

I think about you every single day. To this day, the pain will never go away. I've come to live and accept that what happened was for the good. I just wish people did what they could. You were in the wrong place at the wrong time. You were the blessing that I lost to get away from the crime. The best of a bad bunch; God really takes the best first. That's why your death will always be the worst. You were my best friend. It's just a sad story that your life came to an end. God took you away to take us away from all the temptations. And even now that you're gone I look towards you in complete admiration. Because you were only full of pure intentions. A light in my darkness, May Allah grant you ascension. Ameen. And I hope I can greet you on the other side Insha'Allah. I really hope we can reunite in Jannah. Because I can't wait to tell you my stories. Share everything with you from my mishaps to my glories. I visit you but not often enough, but I know where to find you in the cemetery. And you're buried in the best place, in my memories. You're my brother for eternity and I am grateful that you were in my life. Because you've been with me through the hopelessness and strife. And you'll always be the unforgettable part. The soul that remains in my heart.

- For my friend Imran.

Secrets –

I know what's hidden within you.
The sinister savage nature within
you is one of your closest companions.
Accompanying you with the darkest of sins.
Wicked and vile, if only it could be
a deleted file that could be
extinguished for eternity.

A Peaceful Death –

I just want to repent and receive the redemption I deserve. Because I have a purpose and that is something I constantly serve. I lose track as there are faults all along. Tripping off-course as I tend to be wrong. Choosing the bad path but I regret my past. Perhaps I just can't reveal that half of me because I don't want it to last. I hide it under my clean sleeves. No one needs to know I was tainted when they grieve. I just want then to know that I believe. Never losing my belief even though I wanted to leave. I don't want my corpse to burn. I want forgiveness before I return. I want to pass pleasantly. But that is a myth with my actions presently. I weep because this thought tends to be so deep. I wish to pass peacefully in my sleep.

A Painful Death –

It was so fruitful.
Blossoming fruits that were beautiful.
But it was painted.
Covered in grace that was tainted.
A selfish desire.
One that I wish to retire.
A fire that was evil.
Pretending to be warm as it was lethal.
Burning away fragments.
Halting a treasure that was stagnant.
It used to be so innocent.
But jealousy made it militant.
An immature mind killed it.
A broken heart; lust filled it.
It was shot with a crossbow.
A false comrade was a foe.
Pulling out the arrow.
Crushed bones; absorbing the marrow.
Dehumanising the boy.
Creating a machine; a toy.
Because the heart became dark.
Becoming lost, roaming an empty park.
Thrown under the wheels.
Disregarding how anyone feels.
It was stolen and dropped.
Overfilled and purposely popped.
Now it no longer wants to love.
It lost and now it has had enough.
It gave away everything precious.
Thus, it fell deep into a crevice.
Losing it all and now nothing is left.
The romance within died a painful death.

Suicidal Thoughts Part 1 –

This isn't an easy subject. But it'd be a crime not to reflect. No one understands unless you're in this situation. It haunts me, I want isolation. I can't put on this fake face anymore. I want love but I want space to explore. Searching for my purpose. I need to know why I feel so worthless. I battle with this contemplation of death daily. The demons are watching me struggle for entertainment like the Israelis. I just want someone to care. I want someone to understand the pain I bare. When your closest bond refuses to bother. It feels like the sadness chokes you by the collar. I don't want these tears to fall so freely. I want to be an escapee. I don't want to die as a prisoner. So please, I plead for you to be a listener. I wanted to die, but I want to live. I have so much to do and give. Becoming important to those that show me affection. I just need love, not rejection. Please don't look at me as if I'm insane. I'm just dying to get rid of these chains. I'm sick of the guilt I feel every time I moan. I'm sick of being in a room full of people and feeling alone. Tired of the treacherous torture. Thus, I will climb over these reinforced borders.

Suicidal Thoughts Part 2 –

It's okay, it doesn't have to be this way anymore. Just trust me, you can strengthen your core. It just takes time, be patient. Your soul no longer must be vacant. There are people that care about you, just speak. Talking about it may be hard, but it doesn't make you weak. Remember every time you want to die, there is someone that wants you to be alive. Someone that loves you wants you to thrive. You are not alone, we are together. You are of value, don't think of yourself as any lesser. You are the best person you can possibly be. Only you can express your uniqueness for everyone to see.

Reconstruction

Listen to Your Heart –

Listen to your heart even if it is hard.
You can adjust even if you have the wrong cards.
The mind isn't always right as it can be illogical.
And sometimes the consequences can be diabolical.
Failing to listen defeats the peace.
But listening puts the heart at ease.
Listen to your heart and you'll never regret.
It's not always too late to turn back before fate is set.

I Hate Sin –

I hate it, it's so vile. Making you unworkable like a corrupted file. It ruins the light within, leaving you tainted. Plastering salivating sensations on the screen; an insidious horror that's painted. Tempting you on the surface with sweetness. Enslaving you once it catches a single weakness. Leaving you addicted like a craving methamphetamine addict. Repeatedly reoffending; creating a critical convict. Dangerous to others and yourself. A disgrace to your mother and everybody else. Even if the crimes are concealed; the guilt remains. Each time is another clot of blood on the shirt; a permanent stain. Irremovable as repentance becomes a myth when the heart becomes sealed. Unforgivable because you continue to seek the darkness to be healed. Maybe there is a chance for a change in the final destination. Taking a different turn might find yourself valuable liberation. Freeing yourself from this immortal plague we call sin. With continuous sincere repentance, maybe you'll be granted salvation to win.

Moving On –

You can pick yourself up again; you must create your own might. This strength training will restore your sight. I understand that you loved and you lost. But that doesn't necessarily mean it came at a cost. It doesn't mean that your vision is blurred. And trust me when I say that your prayers will be heard. The pain will subside; you will feel at ease. Inside you'll feel alive, because your soul will never cease. For things to get better, you must keep faith. Otherwise giving up will mean your heart won't be safe. Sometimes it feels like only you are alone in this bubble. But trust me when I say there are so many people like you facing this struggle. And they survive, so you can too. Short term strife is a part of life, but you can get through. Everyone is in your life for a reason, and someone else will enter. That someone will reignite those dying embers.

Rebuild –

I'm so broken down, like a combusted engine.
Strapped in a garage; a temporary detention. The
time runs out so I can be free. Surrounded by a
moat, I'd rather be lost at sea. Because my body is
a boat that never stops sailing. At the same time,
the motor keeps failing. Once I hit the shore, I'll
search for the highest hill. Laying down a fortified
defence to harness my skills. Stacking up the sticks
as an extra layer. Multiple walls of bricks laid down;
invisible from any surveyor. I've been demolished
too many times, but now I'll stand strong. With the
correct foundation, nothing could possibly go
wrong. Rebuilding myself again without my flaws.
Setting the structure correctly so there is stability on
every floor. Building a fire in the core. Feeding wind
into it so it stays raw. Life can wound you till the
blood spilled results in you being killed. You can be
destroyed but it doesn't mean you can't rebuild.

Another Turn –

If only I had another turn with parole. I would prevent the third degree burns on my soul. Avoid the mistakes and learn the lessons from others. Using the trees to shade me rather than the cheap government provided cover. I would live to prevent regret. Acting cautiously so I don't have to forget. Living happily so I don't have to curse. Hurting no one so I make no one feel worse. I just want to restart to be the person I was meant to be. Mentally prepare for the pain that the demons sent to me. Eliminating any threat such as my ignorance. Finding eudaimonia before I meet any hindrance. I would turn back, but at the same time, I would decline. Because God's will is a beautiful thing, who am I to deny any of His signs?

Concealed Brilliance –

Not the best of times; feeling unblessed and
stressed.
Mentally a mess, but I can assure you that you're
blessed.
Contested congestion leaves you to compress; only
to confess.
I must address, that you're forgetting the perfection
you possess.
Eloquently express your excess finesse.
Suppress your ego so that you can progress to
success.
Listen for the mission or face the fact that life has
been written?
Escape the false prison; disperse your wings to be
driven.
Envision ambition; utilise your ability to glisten.
Use precision to make a decision to disregard
division.
Parts may break; it can ache just remain awake.
Ignore the snakes that shake you because they're
fake.
Dreams are set in stone; if need be prevail alone.
Dethrone the crowd and you'll be ready for the
throne.
Breathe the air and flair your strengths and I swear.
The less you care, the less pain you bare.

Perplexed Age –

I developed mentally before those around me.
Aware of all the signs that surround me. Fearing
the reality as everyone else was conditioned.
Maturing ahead of the pack so I'm not politically
positioned. Systematically synchronised to stand in
stupid solidarity. Avoiding austerity as I realised the
social disparities. I couldn't follow the sheep. Too
unique to fall on my knees and weep. Keeping
knowledge treasured because it needed to be
contained. Spreading it where I can, otherwise I
would have complained. I couldn't allow myself to
be a fool. I couldn't stand and watch others become
a tool. For some it was inevitable, but I had to do
my duty. Staying clear of the hypnotism even if it
was juicy. I had to starve myself from temptation.
Only to feed myself of soulful sensations. Maybe
that explains why I always felt socially awkward.
But never will I regret for being forward. As my
beliefs built me into this being. Holding my
principles tightly as I am now the sight that you are
all seeing. I will always be grateful for being older
than my actual age. Granting me the power to
complete each stage.

Coasting –

Let the waves take away the confusion.
Let the leaves take away the pollution.
Just let go of the handle and let the flow
take you wherever it may go.
Life is full of surprises, thus in the face
of adversity, blessing arise.

I Need –

I need peace of the heart,
because I'm sick of the lack
of order breaking it apart.
Give me peace of mind
because I am sick of dying
mentally. Feed me tranquility
please, I need to not be in
pieces. Don't give me love,
I don't want a curse that
constantly hurts. Please,
just give me the realism I
deserve. Please don't have
the nerve to serve me a
notice for severance of my
spinal nerve. I need...
me, myself and you.

A Sense of Relief –

I think maybe now I am finding peace,
and it's so beautiful to feel at ease.
In the desert receiving the cleansing
my soul needs. Even though my skin
bleeds. This feels so essential, feeling
a sense of relief. For once, I feel like I
can finally breathe. I thank God for this
temporary release. I appreciate the
sense of tranquility even though it has
been granted on a lease.

Inner Peace –

Get away from me, run, I beg you. Impeach me like Theresa May because of her bootleg policies. These demons are holding me in captivity with their imperialized colonies. Subjecting me to austerity when I just want inner peace. It is tearing me into particles so that there are missing pieces. It's psychological barbarity, that's preventing my own prosperity. I want tranquility in the heart but all that exists is hostility. No friendly faces, despite the infrequent calm sea, the trading market will always move with volatility. I don't want my blood to rush, please I just want my mind to hush. Flush away this excrement within me, perhaps then I might find purity in my element. I've come to accept my inner peace is a myth as I am permanently in pieces. How can I expect peace without these unreturned leases? These pieces of me that I leased away have perished like Islamic scriptures. Massacred by the Mongols, dumping ink into rivers creating this historical picture.

Phoenix –

Highly ambitious, yet forever superstitious.
A capricious mentality and not the most auspicious.
Actively suspicious of reality so I cast a fantasy.
A pathetic fallacy that has me waiting anxiously.
Casually contain my capacity and decimate
catastrophe.
Frantically falling but I thrive to empower
emphatically.
Success is calling, rising up independently to
progress.
So I shan't regress; ignorance is something I
oppress.
Discarded the chain and disregarded my name.
Started with blame; uncharted myself to reclaim.
The soul; retake control so I'm not stuck in a hole.
Roll up the emptiness; don't let it get parole.
I wish I could exterminate this venomous virus from
my iris.
As I write this, I continue to resist what I miss.
I exist to spread kindness and to bring you out from
the blindness.
Ignore me when I'm spineless but remember these
words are timeless.

Great Things –

Great things entertain great minds hence why your heart sings. Play the heart strings in order to embrace your wings. Driven to the boundary with valiant vision. Powerful precision with the ability to ace any audition. An excellent equestrian to leap over hurdles which is eminent. Exquisitely elegant in your evident element. Talent doesn't die; simply wasted so don't cry. But rather persevere and defy to feel immensely high. Your gift makes you alive; use it to thrive. That deep dive will allow your enlightenment to arrive. Incredibly loyal; humble in such a fashion that makes you royal. Don't let anyone make your blood boil as you're too special to spoil. No one is above you so don't tear up from fear. It's clear; cheer up this is definitely your year. Never forget when you're down that no one will let you drown. A friend will forever change the frown so you can reclaim your crown. Conquer your quest but rest if it hurts your chest. Invest in this test until you've reached your best.

Good Fruits –

The good fruits surround us, but we prefer the rotten. The tempting delicacies that will push us into a coffin. But we need to eat the good fruits to prosper. Anything that is too good to be true is most likely an imposter. Pretending to show a sugar-coated reality. Blatant blasphemy that will never provide true vitality. Cherish the golden opportunities that are offered. Grateful to the point that the bad is bothered. Listen to your heart and you will be given the right suit. Therefore, only ever eat these beautiful good fruits.

God is Near –

He is near, He always will be even when you're in fear. Listening to your heartbeat and catching your every tear. Providing you the struggle to avoid further trouble. Even when the cards shuffle, He won't let you crumble. The help of God is always near; have faith. His mercy is so great; thus, your belief in Him will keep you safe.

Find No Enemy

Broken Dreams -

And these dreams were simply just a fantasy. An unrealistic reality which needs an ambitious amnesty. Hope and energy fuelled each ambition. But they were constantly met with taxed tuition. Teaching the tragedy of tales. Fractured fiction that's lost at sea as it sails. All these broken dreams signify the harshness of living. But, it's softened the soul to learn the art of forgiving. Granting mercy on the loss of goals. Granting acceptance for all of the heartbroken souls. I am simply a damned dreamer living in regret. A volatile wreck that will never forget. Ashamed of my own actions and words. Staring intensively into the mirror, wondering why I am so absurd? Hating every ounce of me because I am at war. Battling myself because the lack of peace has made my heart poor. How could I ever achieve such dreams in this state? A mind which has settled on a futile fate. Perhaps I could change these fragmented dreams through empathy. Altering destiny by educating my identity. Discovering a common ground of equality that has abolished supremacy. Defeating these demons by disregarding demonic ascendancy. Ultimately uniting to Find No Enemy.

Ultimately uniting to
Find No Enemy…

Rayaan Ali -

"A person for the people."

Printed in Great Britain
by Amazon

44562035R00090